Death Goes Digital

How Funeral Directors Can Use LinkedIn To Demonstrate Professionalism, Build Reputation and Create Visibility

By

Peter J. Billingham

Copyright

© 2016 Peter John Billingham

All Rights Reserved

License Notes

No part of this publication may be reproduced, distributed, or transmitted in any form or by any means, including photocopying, recording, or other electronic or mechanical methods, without the prior written permission of the publisher, except in the case of brief quotations embodied in critical reviews and certain other non-commercial uses permitted by copyright law. For permission requests, write to the publisher at info@deathgoesdigital.com

This book is licensed for your personal enjoyment only. This book may not be re-sold or given away to other people. If you would like to share this book with another person, please purchase an additional copy for each person you share it with. If you're reading this book and did not purchase it, or it was not purchased for your use only, then you should return it to Amazon and purchase your own copy. Thank you for respecting the hard work of this author.

Visit:

www.deathgoesdigital.com
www.peterbillingham.com

Child Financial Charity

Financial Support For Families

Child Funeral Charity helps families in England and Wales, who have to arrange a funeral for a baby or a child under 16. Child Financial Charity provides financial support to help with funeral costs, together with practical advice and guidance.

A donation of £1.00 from each paperback copy of this book that is sold will be given to Child Financial Charity to support their work.

For more information on the work of Child Financial Charity, please visit www.childfuneralcharity.org.uk

Follow them on Twitter - @ChildFuneralUK

Contents

DEDICATION vi

ACKNOWLEDGEMENTS vii

WHY SHOULD YOU BUY THIS BOOK? xi

A CAUTIONARY TALE xii

PART 1 - DEATH GOES DIGITAL

INTRODUCTION 2

3 CORE REASONS YOU NEED TO CHANGE 14

DEATH GOES DIGITAL 24

PART 2 - LINKEDIN

WHAT IS LINKEDIN? 32

WHY SHOULD I HAVE A LINKEDIN PROFILE? 41

7 KEY BENEFITS TO HAVING A LINKEDIN PROFILE 47

BUILDING A PERSONAL PROFILE 78

BUILDING A COMPANY PROFILE 84

BUILDING CREDIBILITY THROUGH RECOMMENDATIONS 91

CONCLUSION 96

NEXT STEPS - TAKE ACTION! 100

ABOUT PETER BILLINGHAM 103

RESOURCES 107

NOTES 109

Dedication

To Sam

To the value of cold showers, early mornings and good coffee to pursue in you a spirit of creativity.

Your entrepreneurial drive will take you to places yet undreamed.

I am very proud of you.

To Laura

This calls for a bottle of champagne and a dance on the table. Your tenacious and resilient character is inspiring.

You will make a dent in the world.

I am very proud of you.

Dad

Thank You

> "In normal life we hardly realise how much more we receive than we give, and life cannot be rich without such gratitude. It is so easy to overestimate the importance of our achievements compared with what we owe to the help of others."
>
> Dietrich Bonhoeffer

Each day that passes finds me more grateful. As my life is advancing, growing deeper and older, gratefulness, like opaque cataracts dropping from my eyes, helps me see that people, rather than things, make it richer. I realise all it takes is two words to help others find a deeper purpose and meaning in life. Those two words are "thank you."

There is something most people across the world have in common; that something is the quest to find happiness. We all want to find happiness and discover meaning, purpose and value in our lives. Finding happiness, says Brother David Steindl-Rast[1] a Catholic monk, begins when we start by being grateful for this present moment. This moment is all we have. This moment is a gift. That is why it called the present. The only appropriate response to this moment, he says, is to cultivate and fully experience gratefulness for it. Gratitude is to finding life's purpose as oxygen is to breathing.

Science is proving that people who experience gratefulness have improved health, sleep, better general well-being and self-esteem. What the light of science is now shining down the path towards happiness is what wisdom has beckoned towards for centuries. The eternal truth is that by being grateful first, we then find happiness and not the other way around. Understanding how experiencing gratitude leads to my happiness is helpful. More important is how expressing gratitude can lead to creating happiness for others. All it takes is two words, "thank you."

Thank you, Ray and James Giles, from James Giles & Sons Ltd Funeral Directors in Bromsgrove, Worcestershire. I appreciate the trust and confidence you have in me to serve your clients as a funeral celebrant. To Rachel and the staff team that work with professionalism, care and sensitivity, it is a pleasure and honour to work alongside you all. Thank you for the fun, laughter and teasing. Above all, the example of dedication, commitment and compassion that you give serving those who have lost someone they love. Thank you. And to Neil, who said, "If you don't mention me by name it doesn't count." Well it counts now!

To my life long friend and now editor Terry Bennett. If you opened the dictionary to search for the definition of a best friend, your name would be found there. Thank you.

Thank you to Laura and Sam my amazing children. "If I could line up all the little boys and girls in the world and pick one of each, I'd pick you every time." You are a source of joy in my life. I am extremely proud of you both. Thank you for the support, encouragement and love you give to me to grow and develop new skills. I cannot put into words my love for you both, I wish that all your dreams come true as you experience "a road less travelled" for yourselves. Thank you.

To my wife Noreen, thank you. The grace, love, and care with which you fill each day, makes my life worth living. Thank you for being there in my highest highs and lowest lows. I am and will be eternally grateful that one day many years ago you said, "I do." Thank you.

"The future depends on what you do today."

MAHATMA GANDHI

Why Should You Buy This Book?

There are three compelling questions facing most funeral businesses today.

1. How do I continue to compete and grow my business in an ever-changing, digitally driven marketplace?
2. How will people, who need the services of my business, find our firm when they need a Funeral, Director?
3. How do I move my business more online and not lose the human touch, so important to the funeral industry?

This book focuses on **two key areas** to answer those questions.

1. What is **Digitisation** and how is this impacting the funeral industry.
2. This book explains a logical case for the **benefits** of building a profile on the business social networking platform LinkedIn.

This book is written to encourage action. To do nothing will be a nail in the coffin of your funeral business.

A Cautionary Tale

In a fascinating book called BOLD, Peter Diamandis and Steven Kotler recount the death of Kodak[2]. Kodak died because it failed to take action on the discovery and trend towards digital photography. It had a lingering and painful decline into death. Here is that cautionary tale.

The Death of Kodak

The Eastman Kodak Company began in 1892. George Eastman developed a commercially available camera and supplied the chemicals to develop the film it used. In 1975, Steven Sasson who worked in the research and development at Kodak had spent two years creating the world's first digital still camera. When showing the executives the new invention, he was expecting to hear many questions about how the technology worked. Instead, he heard, Why would anybody want to look at his or her pictures or photographs on an electronic screen? By 1996, Kodak had 140,000 employees and a market capital of $28 billion. They controlled 90% of the film market and 85% of the camera market in the USA. The executives at Kodak ignored an important fact about Digitisation. They ignored the disruptive exponential growth that came along with the impact of the digital transformation of a business.

A disruptive technology, says Diamandis and Kotler, is any innovation that creates a new market and disrupts an existing one. Digital photography disrupted Kodak's business model to the extent that their invention put themselves out of business. By the time Kodak had realised that they could not keep pace with change that Digitisation brought, it was too late. They went bankrupt in January 2012. As the authors prophetically say, "Either disrupt yourself or be disrupted by someone else."[3] Disruptive technology is gaining momentum on the Internet for the funeral industry. Here are just two examples.

Online Funeral Brokers Connecting Customers With Funeral Directors.

Funeralbooker.com launched its new online service in November 2015.[4] An entrepreneurial and professional company set up an easily accessible way for people to book everything needed for a funeral online. Consumers searching online for information about a funeral service can contact them. Then they handle all the details. They offer that funeral to an Independent Funeral Director who has signed up as part of their website. They are like a "middleman" between someone searching online and the funeral industry. Once a client is obtained they then charge a commission to the Funeral Director, who takes the business. It looks a professional site. The model is innovative and will be copied by others in the future. It has significant possibilities for growth in a profitable marketplace.

Your question could be, why are consumers finding and now using this service?

First, because it can be found! When people search for information on the internet about arranging a funeral, their site comes high on the search engine lists. Second, they make the process easy. They take all the planning details away and offer many choices. Finally, they are providing something that many people do not know they can already get at a local Funeral Directors. Why? Because most Funeral Directors websites are full of features. Full of pictures of staff next to shiny limousines. They do not have the customer focused approach of a firm like www.funeralbooker. Will this work? Probably so. There are upsides. If you are the only Funeral Director in the area on www.funeralbooker you could get more business. The downside, you will not make as much profit per funeral.

Funeral Directors Price Comparison Sites

Funeral debt is a growing problem. The cost of funerals has risen by 88% in the last 10 years according to the annual Sun Life report.[5] In a 2014 report by Royal London, they claim that the total funeral debt in the UK is a round £142m.[6] This increasing cost of funerals will be a key factor driving clients to search the internet for price information about funerals. Today people are familiar with a price comparison site for buying car or house insurance. We input the details and up comes a variety of companies with their prices. Two companies offering the same services for the funeral industry are www.comparethecoffin.com and www.funeralcomparison.co.uk. Type in a postcode and appropriate information and on screen is a list of various services to buy. Again, a local Funeral Director can do the same. However, people who search the Internet first probably will not get to a Funeral Directors website. Even comparethemarket.com one of the UK's leading price comparison sites has a page with a guide to funeral costs! I wonder if you get a fluffy meerkat with every funeral?

Where Does This Leave The Traditional Funeral Director?

Some of the online models above will come and go; that is a given. What should make a Funeral Director sit up and take notice is the number of such options increasing online every day. It is easy to scoff. It is easy to say it will not affect the Funeral Industry. People will always want to deal with the human touch of a local firm, say many Funeral Directors. The first digital camera was the size of a toaster. It weighed 8.5 pounds and had a resolution of 0.01 megapixels. The iPhone 6 Plus weighs 6.07 ounces. It can record still images at up to 43 megapixels, video at 1080HD and, amazingly, you can make phone calls on it! That only took 25 years to happen. The speed of technology has vastly increased the pace of change. It is not hard to believe that every industry, including the funeral industry, will be disrupted by Digitisation. As Diamandis and Kotler say, the first technological threats seem laughingly insignificant. However, for many industries that laughter has turned into tears. Will that happen to the Funeral Industry? Time will tell. But for certain, the marketplace will be disrupted.

When many people read a book such as this, they are often confused about what to do first. That confusion can lead to procrastination. Doing nothing is not an option. If you are in the funeral profession, you must become aware of the disruption that Digitisation is bringing. You must take action to move your business in the direction of change. Failure to take action is to bury your head in the sand. To imagine that it will all go away. Or that people will not adapt to the new digital reality of the funeral profession. Kodak did that and went bankrupt in the process! It is a cautionary tale with a sting in it. "Either disrupt yourself or be disrupted by someone else."

PART ONE – DEATH GOES DIGITAL

Introduction

CHANGE

To Change - an action or method through which something becomes different.

"Here's to the crazy ones. The misfits. The rebels. The troublemakers. The round pegs in the square holes. The ones who see things differently. They're not fond of rules. And they have no respect for the status quo. You can quote them, disagree with them, glorify or vilify them. About the only thing you can't do is ignore them. Because they **change** things. They push the human race forward. And while some may see them as the crazy ones, we see genius. Because the people who are crazy enough to think they can **change** the world, are the ones who do."[7]

Who Is This Book For?

- It is for owners of Independent Funeral Directors
- It is for the CEO's of small Independent Funeral Directors Groups
- It is for the Leadership and Managers of National Independent Funeral Directors Associations
- It is for Marketing Directors of National Funeral Organisations
- It is for branch managers, office managers and staff in national Funeral Service companies.
- It is for businesses who market their products and services to the funeral industry.

This book is for those who see that the marketplace of the funeral industry is changing. It is for those who see this development, but are unsure what to do first. This book is for those who are willing to change. It is for those firms willing to adapt to this shift in society. It is for those who wish to embrace digital marketing and social media to attract new customers.

Throughout this book the term "you" is referring to the audiences above. Not everything covered in this book will be relevant in all cases. This situation is true in many things in life. So it is true when considering digital strategies for the funeral industry. My intention is not to provide answers to every question on digital networking. But to set the process in motion. It is to ask, "What can digital marketing do for your funeral business?"

What Could This Book Do For Your Funeral Business?

In a 2015 white paper from The Economist titled, Digital Evolution, Learning From The Leaders In Digital Transformation,[8] 444 leading executives from varying global industries declared that Digitisation was a major factor changing their businesses. Digitisation is the process of converting systems and processes into a digital or online format. The overriding factor driving the digital transformation of their businesses was evolving customer expectations. The sophistication of digital consumer technologies such as smartphones and social media platforms means that customers have high expectations for their digital interaction with businesses. The report describes businesses by their behaviour as either being ahead of the curve of change or behind the curve. Where is your funeral business? Are you ahead of the curve of Digitisation or behind? Did you even know that such a curve existed?

This book is written to introduce the subject of the Digitisation of a funeral business. It highlights some of the trends impacting the funeral industry as the wave of Digitisation engulfs the traditional operation of many funeral businesses. To ignore or to try to hold back these trends is like King Canute trying to hold back the waves. It just cannot happen. These waves of change have already washed upon the shores of the funeral industry. The tide is coming in fast!

This book could help you make one of the first steps in the right direction of Digitising your funeral business. The subject of Digitisation is vast and covers many areas. For more information, resources and consulting advice on bringing digital systems into your funeral business visit the Death Goes Digital blog or podcast at www.deathgoesdigital.com . For more information on learning about LinkedIn see the reference section.

What Is This Book About?

This book aims to show how Digitisation can be used with regards to one of many platforms to market a business online. This book is written to encourage, educate and engage Funeral Directors to consider the business social network LinkedIn. This book is not a comprehensive explanation of LinkedIn. [9] There are many books or resources on the features of LinkedIn that you could buy. There are so many creative ways that you can use LinkedIn that a book this size could not cover them all. This book explains **why** LinkedIn should be the platform of choice to start a digital strategy for a funeral business. There will be some sections here, however, that are only covered at surface level.

This book is about the **benefits** a LinkedIn profile can achieve for your business.

There is a big difference between **features** and **benefits**.

- **Features** - These are statements about what a product or service is. How it works, what it does and specific aspects of its operation.

- **Benefits** - These are statements about what a product or service will do for its user. The value they will gain from the product or service.

Understanding this difference could mean a client choosing your funeral business over another firm. From my observation, many funeral businesses have websites full of **features**. A list of features does not make the business stand out enough. They fail to show how their business differs from other funeral businesses. People are then driven by the only question left, how much? Choice dictated by price only.

Price only is not effective for anyone. It creates a flow of customers only chasing prices. It reduces the profitability and sets service standards by the wayside. The right words on a website can explain the **benefits** of your firm. It takes the conversation away from price to focus it on what makes your business unique. That is what people will buy. People buy people first. People buy a service for what they can **benefit**, not what **features** that service has. What are the USP's (unique selling points) about your funeral firm? Your unique selling points convince a potential customer you have something different to offer. LinkedIn gives you an opportunity to market your USP's online before someone contacts your firm.

This book covers the **benefits** of including LinkedIn into your digital strategy. It explains how LinkedIn builds an online presence that can drive customers to your business.

Important Disclaimer: This is not an "overnight success" or "quick fix" strategy. It is not a guaranteed method of

7

success. Starting this course of action today will not lead to more customers tomorrow! There is little in the business world that can. Most business owners understand it takes effort, time and persistence to build any business. It is exactly the same with developing a digital strategy. It will take 12 to 18 months before you start to see significant traction online. All social media platforms are the same. It is the consistent online engagement that builds momentum. There is no longer a choice for funeral businesses to ignore their online reputation. The longer your firm waits before it embraces these changes, the further it will get behind the curve. The marketplace is shifting. Innovative firms are fully embracing the digital landscape of the funeral industry.

The funeral industry is a professional and specialist area. I am not a Funeral Director. I am a registered funeral celebrant that officiates at funerals most weeks. I have worked with many conscientious and dedicated Funeral Directors both Independent and from National organisations. A Funeral Director is a complex, multi-skilled and challenging role. Dedicated staff in local Funeral Directors and National organisations provide a wonderful service. Very few people understand the difficult situations they face everyday. My admiration goes to those who provide this care and support in an highly emotional situation.

My background involves leading a number of International charities where developing a digital strategy was central to the marketing strategy. I built and lead creative teams in developing content online to drive millions of clients to websites and then to take action on the information presented. This involved social media, online TV and radio, and podcasting. It is the connection of these two areas, understanding how Digitisation works and working in the funeral industry, that I can offer advice and encouragement to bring about change.

Will reading this book guarantee digital marketing success? Will it guarantee that your funeral business stays ahead of the curve? No. If I said it would, it would be a lie. This book will promise that if you read, and take action on the ideas enclosed, you will move ahead in building your business presence online. The Internet is here to stay. It will impact your business. It will impact your funeral business in drastic ways that you can't yet imagine or even believe. Start by making the changes your business needs by starting to build a LinkedIn profile today. Is this all you need to do? Not by a long shot! But the journey of a 1000 miles begins with one step. Get moving!

Losing a loved one is a difficult and challenging time. People want to find answers. Families want to know about your funeral business. Traditional methods of advertising such as directories may have been effective in the past. But importantly, how will the potential customers of tomorrow find you in a digital friendly world? What about families who are moving into your town or city from other locations? Why would they choose your business over one of your competitors? What is it about your business that **Demonstrates Professionalism, Builds Reputation,** and **Creates Visibility?**

A funeral business grew and expanded in towns and cities by reputation and tradition. Family businesses built up trust and awareness in a community. They did this serving many generations of local families. When great grandad passed away, they chose your family business. It would be likely then when grandad or other members of the family passed they would still choose your business. Today, families rarely stay in the one location. For example, moving to university or employment relocation cause a family to spread out across the country. When requiring the services of a Funeral Director no longer will a scan of the local newspaper be normal. The question remains as to what will be enough for them to find and choose your business?

The Days of The Newspaper Advert Have Gone

When we have a question or want to find the services of a business, any business, we let our "fingers do the walking." No longer do they walk across bright yellow coloured directories. Today, we reach for a computer or a smartphone and "Google it." Not that long ago that phrase would mean nothing, now it is part of the lexicon of normal life. You can be sure your future customers will type into a search bar, "I need a Funeral Director [town]." Where they find, the answer to that question will dictate if your business will get the order. Competition in the funeral sector is growing. More options for funeral services are available than ever before. Even local councils are now considering operating funeral companies.[10] To rely just on the tradition of the family name and a newspaper ad each week to drive sales will become obsolete.

To not have a presence on the internet is no longer a choice. Most businesses understand this, so they have a website. Many funeral businesses stop at this point in a building and thinking about how they will be found on the internet. A website with text and pictures of shiny hearses with black coated staff will no longer suffice. Those days have long past. If your business wants to attract new customers in the future, you will need a mobile responsive website, (a website that is developed to be seen on a mobile phone) that has clear calls to action and is simple to navigate. Alongside these mandatory components is a relevant presence on social media.

When people think of social media, usually Facebook or Twitter comes to mind. These platforms have distinct uses. In future books and ebooks we will explain how a funeral business can use these platforms in a relevant and sensitive way. But one networking site should take priority for a funeral business. That is the business networking platform LinkedIn. This book explains a logical case for the **benefits** as an individual and as a business being on LinkedIn.

This book is a starting point and a basic guide to the subject of using LinkedIn as a Funeral Director. This book concentrates on the UK market. This resource is ideal for the owner or manager of a funeral business. It is also of benefit to anyone that works in the funeral services industry. It is not necessary for you to have a knowledge of computing to be effective using LinkedIn. Yet, there things are important to note.

- It will take time to establish a personal and company profile.
- It will take time to keep content relevant and updated.
- It will take time to understand all the opportunities available.

There Are Seven Key Benefits For Your Business To Use LinkedIn

By the time that you have completed reading this book you will understand and be able to explain:

- What LinkedIn is and **seven key** reasons how it will bring **benefits** to your funeral business.

These are just starting points. Taking action and establishing a LinkedIn profile will put you ahead in the race to take the funeral industry into a digital age. It does take time to set up a LinkedIn account, but some of these time-consuming tasks can be outsourced. You can pay an agency to create and write a LinkedIn profile for you and your business. The outsourcing cost of setting up a LinkedIn account could be the same as paying for three or four months adverts in a local paper, but are online 24 hours of every day! For more information how you could outsource building a profile as well as other aspects of a building a digital marketing strategy, see the reference section.

LinkedIn will be working for your business 24 hours a day 365 days a year. What will is do for your funeral business? A

LinkedIn account **Demonstrates Professionalism, Builds Reputation** and **Creates Visibility.**

So let's get started on the process of taking your funeral business to a new level of digital marketing using LinkedIn.

3 Core Reasons You Need To Change

"The arrogance of success is to think that what you did yesterday will be sufficient for tomorrow."

WILLIAM POLLARD

3 Core Reasons You Need To Change

Change takes effort. Whenever we want to move forward in our lives or our businesses, we need to change. One of my favourite change quotes is by the famous car maker Henry Ford.

"If you always do what you've always done, you'll always get what you've always got."

Do you want different results? Then you need to change your actions. According to Einstein, insanity is "doing the same thing over and over again and expecting different results." Change is never easy. We get comfortable in our ways. We get familiar with systems. We get used to things as they are. Change can make us uncomfortable and insecure. We can also get into a rut. We can be like an ostrich and bury our heads in the sand and believe that things will always stay the same. We can talk about the "good old days" and hear that classic line, "we've always done it this way!" The reality is we may not feel comfortable with change. But change is here to stay! Business is changing. It is changing extremely fast running a business in a digital world.

Recently, I was watching my two-year-old nephew playing with an iPhone. He sat on the floor flicking through photographs, stretching images and pressing different icons. Playing with this "toy," that could make noises and show pretty pictures, was intuitive. He will grow up with a digital mindset. There are still a few people who remember a mouse is an animal, and a window is something you open to let air in! For most the vocabulary of today however, would immediately bring to mind something completely different. This move towards an online life will not change back, it will only increase and impact more and more of our lives.

Change through choice is far better, than by force. In every industry, profession and marketplace, the Internet has created tsunami waves of change. Understanding this change is a critical area where Funeral Directors need to be aware of shifts in culture. How do you change by choice? How do you change your strategy and action? How will funeral businesses prepare for the continuing pace of change? These are pressing questions that Funeral Directors need to answer. Understanding why something needs to change is as important as what to change. If there is a big enough "why" then it generates enough effort to overcome the inertia that holds us back.

There are three core reasons how building a LinkedIn profile positively impacts a funeral services business. Using LinkedIn can:

- Demonstrate **Professionalism**
- Build **Reputation**
- Create **Visibility**

Let's explore in more detail these three core reasons and how they impact your business.

Professionalism

"Professionalism is like love: it is made up of the constant flow of little bits of proof that testify to devotion and care."
Tomislav Šola

We do not become professionals overnight. To be a professional in any area of life, in business or sport, takes dedication, time and effort. Being a professional involves demonstrating many "bits of proof." These "bits of proof" build a detailed picture of your business to prospective clients one piece at a time. The definition of professionalism is:

"The competence or skill expected of a professional, the conduct, aims, or qualities that characterise or mark a profession or a professional person."[11]

How do you demonstrate to potential customers the competence, skill and qualities that mark you and your firm as professional? Where can you display these "bits of proof?" Legislation does not currently regulate the UK funeral industry. The debate surrounding the benefits of regulation has many positives and negatives. How you establish your business as professional is critical now that clients have access to more information online. Establishing professionalism is vital when someone wants to choose a Funeral Director. Families need to be confident in the training, experience, and the quality of service you will offer. Your website needs to describe how professionalism is an integral to your business. Demonstrating membership of national associations such as the NAFD or SAIF and how you work in line with their codes of practice is vital.

The benefits of a LinkedIn profile **Demonstrates Professionalism** in a digital marketplace. Being absent on the world's largest network of professionals and businesses does not.

A LinkedIn profile **Demonstrates Professionalism** in a simple and cost-effective way for your funeral business.

Reputation

"You can't build a reputation on what you are going to do."
— Henry Ford

The reputation of many Funeral Directors today stands on the shoulders of previous family generations. Establishing that reputation has taken a lifetime or even many lifetimes. How we communicate that reputation though, is changing. Reputation is spread by word of mouth. It is a sad fact that news of bad customer service reaches twice as many ears as praise for good service.[12] It is obvious we need to do whatever is possible to avoid negative comments. It also obvious you should do everything you can to find ways to highlight positive recommendations. The definition of the word reputation is:

"The estimation in which a person or thing is held, especially by the community or the public generally."[13]

Managing the reputation of your business was once just a local community affair. This is no longer the case. We live in an age where reviews from other people, influence our purchasing decisions. Think Tripadvisor. Finding ways to give potential customers feedback on the service already provided is important. There is now a whole industry developed around the idea of reputation management[14] for your business.

In the past, hiring a public relations firm could have helped build the persona and reputation of a business. In this digital age, it is a different situation. You now need to pay attention to establishing, keeping and protecting your online reputation. What are people saying about your business on the Internet? Do you even know?

On LinkedIn, it is possible to receive recommendations and endorsements demonstrating and building your online reputation. Rather than this be a reactive approach, LinkedIn gives the opportunity to be proactive and create recommendations. Building a LinkedIn profile will benefit your online reputation.

A LinkedIn profile helps **Build Reputation** in a simple and cost-effective way for your funeral business.

Visibility

"The power of visibility can never be under estimated." Margaret Cho

How visible is your funeral service business in your local community?

Not far from where I lived as a boy was a funeral services business. It had a large granite sign outside its premises. It was a dark foreboding place where we would dare each other to go and look. I don't know what we expected to have find had we the courage to look through those dark and frosted windows! The building had a certain feel to it that was not good. It was not the kind of place that you would have gone just to ask questions. That was unless you needed the service of an undertaker or stonemason!

Engaging the services of a Funeral Director is the task that most people fear. Death is part of life. But it does not make the process any easier. Funeral Directors have gone to great lengths to break down these barriers. Offices now create a much softer, customer focused environment. However, there is still the need to engage with sensitivity those seeking out funeral services. The rise of prepaid funeral plans create an opportunity to make choices about our end of life plans. This is now a personal decision, rather than by a family following the death of a loved one. To be visible is no longer just about being available when someone has passed away. It is about creating an online presence that is engaging, open and transparent. A place where people feel able to contact you and discuss an area that was once almost taboo.

Visibility is defined as "The state of being able to see or be seen."[15]

To just be <u>seen</u> in a local community through newspaper advertising is no longer enough. If a potential customer searches the Internet of your area have you have done everything that you can to be seen online? This should include a strategic digital marketing plan. This means building a platform of mobile response websites, and social media profiles. Adding into this strategic plan LinkedIn, however, increases your visibility considerably through web searches.

These three core reasons tie together why a funeral services business needs to use LinkedIn. Using LinkedIn can help your business:

- **Demonstrate Professionalism**
- **Build Reputation**
- **Create Visibility**

In the next chapter, we will explore how the marketplace is changing through Digitisation, how death has now gone digital!

Chapter Questions and Thought Provokers

- What is your view about change, is this something that you embrace or reject?
- Do you say, "we've always done it this way!" or "What opportunities could this change bring to my business?"
- Can you identify with the quote from the Apple advertising campaign, are you a misfit?
- With number 1 being, "I've never heard of digital marketing and social media." And 10 being, "Mark Zuckerberg and I are best friends," how would you rate your knowledge on this subject?
- How often do you update your website?
- When was the last time you checked all the links on your website to make sure they are active and correct?
- What social media platforms do you use privately and which for business?
- What are the **benefits** of doing business with your firm?
- What are the USP's of your funeral business?
- What pictures do the words Professionalism, Reputation and Visibility conjure up in your mind?

Death Goes Digital

"They always say time changes things, but you actually have to change them yourself."

ANDY WARHOL

Death Goes Digital

How is the Internet Changing The Funeral Industry?

Mankind has always mourned the dead. A fascinating infographic from USA Today[16] charts the way we have memorialised the dead. It describes how death notices first appeared in magazines in the 1700s. It explains how over time these notices included photographs and then detailed biographies. In recent times, the funeral service of Princess Diana and Pope John Paul II brought the world to a stop. Millions around the globe shared in the mourning for the loss of these lives. From the late 1900s, the rise of the Internet gives new and global ways to share the memorial of a deceased loved one. New digital businesses such as legacy.com[17] have created enormous databases of obituary and memorial notices. 24 million unique visitors from around the world log on each month to the website. Legacy.com is currently hosting around 20 million obituaries. To share the loss of a loved one, social media sites give people a new environment for their expression of loss. This may still seem strange today. Tomorrow it will seem normal.

The Internet gives more access to discussions and news about death and dying than ever before. National organisations like Dying Matters [18] are bringing the conversation of death to public attention.[19] Entrepreneurial Funeral Directors that are ahead of the curve are developing creative ways to build the visibility of their business. C.P.J. Field & Co Ltd recently appointed Hannah Sherriffs as a

"Writer In Residence."[20] They are the first Funeral Directors in the UK to try this. It is a creative bid to break down the social barriers associated with the topic of death. They post blog updates and will collate all this material into an e-book at the end of the first year. It will be interesting to see how this development grows and benefits their customers. In the near future many Funeral Directors will follow suit with blog posts, podcasts, YouTube channels and the like. It will happen. It is happening.[21]

The University of Bath, Centre for Death & Society, is bringing academic insight on the subject of death going digital.[22] Their extensive research on social networks and technology provides new thinking and processes to deal with loss and mourning. The Internet and digital technology provides applications now considered normal and routine for Funeral Directors. Accessing the Wesley Music system in crematoriums, filing reports and collecting charitable donations. These advances make a Funeral Directors work simpler and faster because death has gone digital. The future development of even more bespoke mobile apps will revolutionise the funeral industry.[23]

One of the growing issues facing society today is the subject of digital legacy.[24] What happens to the digital assets of the deceased person? Have they left passwords? Have they left access to online accounts? Online financial accounts like PayPal or entertainment accounts such as betting or bingo? What are their wishes about what happens to their Facebook account? We have never had to consider these issues in the past but death going digital forces us to ask new questions.

The wide and important subject of digital mourning and digital legacy needs covering in a separate book. This fascinating aspect of modern culture is changing at a pace so fast that it is difficult to comment relevantly as it changes everyday. It is a pressing issue that National Organisations and local Funeral Directors can not ignore anymore. Death has gone digital!

Chapter Questions and Thought Provokers

- How has the internet impacted your business?
- What internet tools (email, calendars, CRM - the client database) do you use?
- How could your client interaction be enhanced using online methods?
- Which online donation collection websites are you using for your clients in memorial giving?
- What options are you providing clients to establish online tributes?
- What questions do your clients ask about online obituaries?
- Why do you think people are able to talk about death through initiatives like Dying Matters?
- How could your business build on the wave of the growth of death cafes?
- How many of your clients now use the Wesley Music system over traditional organ music?
- What issues surrounding digital legacies are starting to raise questions with your clients?

PART TWO – LINKEDIN

What Is LinkedIn?

"You never change things by fighting the existing reality. To change something, build a new model that makes the existing model obsolete."

R. BUCKMINSTER FULLER

What Is LinkedIn?

Launched in 2003, LinkedIn is the number one professional, business-focused global social networking site. As with many tech start-ups, Reid Hoffman began the company in his living room around a coffee table. Then it was the realm of science fiction, but now it is common for people to communicate by mobile phone with business colleagues around the world. Nobody considers that unusual. We know that businesses soon adapt to significant advances in technology. The vision Reid Hoffman imagined of business networking in a digital age is now a reality. I cannot imagine he would ever have believed LinkedIn could play such a critical role in businesses online. LinkedIn constantly develops to the changing requirements of doing business in a digital media environment. [25] Many of the features and options on LinkedIn have come and gone. However, the core ideas behind its establishment remain.

The question is, does it have value for you and your business as a Funeral Director?

- What are the **benefits** for a Funeral Director to build a profile on LinkedIn?
- Could investing time on LinkedIn impact your funeral business?
- Does LinkedIn have a place in the digital strategy for a Funeral Director alongside a website?

The answer to all those questions and many more is a positive and resounding yes! It will take time, effort and frequent attention to gain valuable benefits from LinkedIn. In return, if you invest the time, your business will demonstrate professionalism, build reputation and create visibility showing you are relevant in this digital age. You will build your reputation as clients, and networking partners view your recommendations. Creating visibility, will give insight to your business online as Funeral Director.

There are **three key benefits** to building a profile on the platform according to LinkedIn.[26]

- **Connect - Find - Be found** These three will build your professional identity online and stay in touch with colleagues.

The subject of death and bereavement is in the media more than ever before. In the past, death was considered a taboo subject to engage conversation around. The reality has been the mortality rate for human beings hovers around 100%! We all know that death is a part of living. We have death thrust in our faces every day through the news, movies or in books. It can seem it always happens to someone else. Until one day that stark reality is an issue with which we have to deal. In most situations today when people need information they open the search bar in Google. When people type "Funeral Director [town]" into their computers is your business seen? What page number does it appear? Have you checked? Creating a professional image LinkedIn gives you transparent points of contact for potential clients. A profile on LinkedIn shows, for example, how your firm retains independence from national conglomerates. LinkedIn establishes your professional reputation in your community. It allows you to build networks with doctors, nursing homes, hospices and other businesses online.

- **Learn and Share** - Get the latest news, inspiration and insights about your industry.

One of the more recent benefits of investing time on LinkedIn is accessing up to date knowledge. You can gain new ideas and keep up-to-date with thought leaders in your field. LinkedIn gives information on news and trends in the funeral industry. Do you want to be seen as a thought leader in the industry? Do you want to show your knowledge, skill and professionalism to a wider audience? Do you want to showcase charitable efforts and community involvement? LinkedIn gives you a professional platform to establish your credibility and reputation. Not only in your local community, but also through national networks. Sharing news about your activity and knowledge can be done simply, regularly and directly

- **Power your career** - Discover professional opportunities, business deals and new ventures.

You may not be considering a new employer, yet we all know that circumstances change. This may not be at the forefront of your mind now. A professional LinkedIn profile describing your abilities, training and skills could be of benefit in the future. It is now normal for employers and recruitment agencies looking for staff to start with a LinkedIn search. This is how employers of the future will find you.

Each one of these three key aspects will be covered in more detail in the following chapters.

How Is The UK Funeral Industry Represented On LinkedIn?

By using a simple search,[27] 985 UK LinkedIn profiles have Funeral Director in their job title. There are 323 companies that have funeral as part of their business description. This includes Funeral Directors, celebrants, and every possible business connected to the funeral industry. Filter down deeper, and only 58 businesses that are individuals or family-owned are listed. An office of fair trading report estimates that there are around 4000 Funeral Directors in the UK.[28] This includes national organisations such as the Co-op or Dignity. Even with this simple surface level survey there is great potential available for those businesses who start using digital marketing. Some may say there is little representation because there is no need. Some would say this perhaps "Luddite" mentality says the funeral industry is not an area necessary for a digital presence. This opinion is not valid in a fully digital age. We are only on the cusp where the world of death and digital will continue to collide. Now is the opportunity to move ahead! Firms willing to engage with customers digitally will be the firms of the future who gain the market share. Is your firm ready for Digitisation?

This chapter gives a brief overview of the origins, purpose and current use of LinkedIn. Now we turn to the critical question of why a Funeral Director needs a professional LinkedIn profile.

Who uses LinkedIn?

LinkedIn is a social networking site designed for the business community. If you are an owner or managing a Funeral Directors, it is important that you have a profile on LinkedIn. LinkedIn initially was used by those seeking employment opportunities and to build a network of people they knew and trust. These are still two excellent benefits from building a network through LinkedIn. These only scratch the surface of the potential impact you can have as a Funeral Director. LinkedIn is a place for other professionals to connect with you and for you to be viewed as a professional to others. As the Internet develops, the needs of businesses in a digital world have expanded. LinkedIn now offers huge potential beyond its original format.

LinkedIn offers a basic free membership option. This allows you to build professional "connections" as a opposed to say, "friends." You can make connections with somebody you have done business with or know. This could be online or offline. Alternatively, you can connect with someone with whom you have had a previous networking relationship. A premium subscription offers significant benefits of accessing a range of contacts in LinkedIn. However, for most Funeral Directors the free membership options would be more than enough.

How many people are using LinkedIn?

- There are more than 347 million registered members around the world.

- More than 17 million registered members are from the United Kingdom.
- LinkedIn has members in more than 200 different countries.
- LinkedIn is available in 24 languages.
- 2 people a second join LinkedIn[29]

What are the ways that people are using LinkedIn?[30]

- 81% are using the services of the free LinkedIn account.
- 75% of the users have 500 connections or less.
- 50% of users are members of up to 20 groups.
- 43% of users spend less than two hours a week developing their LinkedIn network.
- 26% of users spend between three and four hours a week developing their LinkedIn network.
- 75% of users found one of the most helpful features was the opportunity to see who had viewed your profile.
- 36% of users say that LinkedIn has been important in developing their business.

For a review on LinkedIn across the world, the research company DMR provides stats, training, and further data. They go to great lengths to support the importance that this social networking platform provides the business world.[31]

Chapter Questions and Thought Provokers

- Have you registered with LinkedIn?
- How many business networking relationship do you have?
- What method do you use to store contacts for business?
- What benefits could you receive from building a LinkedIn profile?
- When do you gather with other industry professionals to discuss the latest issues you are facing ?
- Have you searched "Funeral Director [town]?"
- Where does your business appear in the rankings? (Sign out of your search engine provider first)
- What trade information sources do you currently use?
- If you wanted to recruit new staff or find career opportunities where would you start searching?
- What is your opinion about the funeral industry using social media and the internet to grow its awareness in a community?

Why Should I Have A LinkedIn Profile?

"The only way to make sense out of change is to plunge into it, move with it, and join the dance."

ALAN W. WATTS

Why Should I Have A LinkedIn Profile?

- Do you sit around the office with nothing to do thinking how you can fill your day with more work?
- Do you long to have yet another task on your ever expanding "to do list?"
- Do you have any free time to think about growing your business?

The answer to those questions is usually a resounding no! From my experience, most Funeral Directors have enough work on their desk to keep them busy for days! There is always a difficult balance between "Urgent" and "Important" tasks. The phone rings chasing urgent outstanding issues. Funeral Directors are urgently contacting crematoriums and churches, looking after families, dealing with suppliers or waiting for doctors reports to fill their day. These issues press on us. They seem urgent, a ringing phone often does! It can lead to little time being available for the "Important, but not "Urgent" activities of the business. Why would adding to that workload by creating a LinkedIn Profile help your business?

Marketing your business is an "Important" or essential activity. It is an activity that gets sidelined by the "Urgent." However, it is critical for the long-term success and profitability of any business. Many Funeral Directors rely on traditional methods for marketing and obtaining new business. This includes advertising in local newspapers and national directories. Maybe sponsorship of local events and adverts in a local church and hospital magazines. Funeral

Directors spend considerable amounts of money by advertising weekly in local free papers. Are these methods of marketing still as successful as they once were? Will they continue to remain so?

The latest trends in accessing news information reveal the value of newspapers for advertising. A 2014 OFCOM [32] report said newspaper readership declined rapidly in the last ten years. In particular, among the under 35s. During the same period, people who accessed news on the Internet increased substantially. This gives an indication of how people now want to receive news. Local newspaper replicate the same trends.

How Effective Is Traditional Advertising?

Ian Burrell in the Daily Telegraph writes, "The latest print circulation figures for Britain's regional newspapers appear to show an industry driven to the precipice and staring at imminent extinction." [33] The local newspapers that are succeeding and growing readers, he says, are those providing news on the Internet alongside a print version. This brief insight demonstrates the way people want and now search for information. The trend will continue to decline in the readership of local papers. How effective will that weekly advert you place remain and what is the alternative? How can you spend time doing the "Important but not "Urgent" task of marketing your business? It requires the same activity for your funeral business that successful local newspapers employ - building an internet profile alongside the tradition print forms of marketing.

An updated, mobile responsive website is indispensable for a Funeral Director. Also, a profile on LinkedIn provides a 24 hour a day business marketing opportunity.

Having a LinkedIn profile benefits your business in 7 key ways.

A profile on LinkedIn -

1. Establishes credibility and trust.
2. Guides clients to choose your firm.
3. Creates growing business networks.
4. Identifies you as a "thought leader" in the funeral industry.
5. Helps sell you before selling your company.
6. Helps You Respond To Changing Trends
7. Allows you to be active in professional communities.

LinkedIn is an effective and targeted way to connect to the right people, at the right time and in the right way. It provides a online platform for your business to build its reputation and reach new clients for free. LinkedIn is the complete solution to business networking.

Let's now look in detail at each one of these key benefits a LinkedIn account will bring your funeral business.

Chapter Questions and Thought Provokers

- How much time do you spend working "on" your business or working "in" your business?
- What is your strategy to grow or maintain the profile of your business in your community?
- What would you categorise as "Important" but not Urgent" in your business right now?
- If you suddenly gained an extra day to spend growing your business, what would you do?
- How effective is your current advertising efforts?
- What impact is your current marketing campaign having?
- How can your prove or measure this success?
- What is your annual budget for advertising?
- Why do you keep putting adverts in the local paper?
- Which of the 7 ways LinkedIn could benefit your business interests you the most?

7 Key Benefits To Having A LinkedIn Profile

"To improve is to change; to be perfect is to change often."

WINSTON S. CHURCHILL

7 Key Benefits To Having A LinkedIn Profile

1. A LinkedIn Profile Establishes Credibility and Trust

The funeral industry has changed drastically over the last 20 - 30 years. There was a time that almost all funeral businesses were long-established family-owned firms. Serving a local area, they traded on reputation, tradition and word-of-mouth referrals. A medium sized town could support a small number of funeral businesses. They all knew each other and had existed side by side for perhaps two or three generations of the family.

The Marketplace Has Shifted

New independent, creative and forward thinking entrepreneurial funeral businesses have opened. Regional Funeral Directors trading under the name of previous family owned businesses are expanding. Add into this mix national organisations. Firms such as Dignity Caring Funerals who often keep the old family business name. The Co-operative Funeral Care whose "shops" are on the High Street. That can make it difficult for clients to know sometimes who owns the business. It can be a confusing marketplace. This uncertainty will drive client to search for information on the Internet.

This is not all bad news; competition can be good. Transparency in business creates trust. For a family, recently bereaved, in turmoil, knowing about the value, support and service you can offer brings a difficult choice. Why should they choose **your** firm over another in the area?

We know that consumers do not only buy on price alone, but other factors are also important to drive the decision. The Internet provides the opportunity to seek reviews of services and products. [34] People now buy on the recommendation of others. Online reviews where service, professionalism and customer care matters often influence over price. This is where the value of a professional, comprehensive and up to date LinkedIn profile can help. LinkedIn allows a Funeral Director to establish credibility and trust through business transparency. Many recommendations from satisfied customers create confidence. Displaying industry qualifications adds to the Funeral Directors credibility. Membership of NAFD or SAIF, for example, show commitment to abide by a code of practice. This offers reassurance and trustworthiness. Some people may not understand what these membership associations offer. A simple paragraph on your LinkedIn profile can educate customers to understand your business. Describing the history and business status provides clarity and openness all that further increases trust.

Would regulation of the UK funeral industry be a good or bad thing? Would the consumer benefit? There are many sides to the argument. For now, consumers are becoming more aware of searching for information. Customers want reviews about the products and services they need to buy. Customers want transparency. The benefit of a LinkedIn profile allows you to do this and establish credibility and trust online.

2. A LinkedIn Profile Helps Clients Choose Your Firm

- How do clients find your firm when they are looking for a Funeral Director?
- What choices cause someone to choose your firm over another Funeral Director in the area?
- What makes your funeral services firm unique?

Where do you search for answers to questions these days? Most people start that quest by typing the question into a search engine. Google even offers that process by voice. Just ask Google or Siri a question and it will give you a list of answers. Families now use this process when looking for a Funeral Director. Even in emotional turmoil, people still research their questions by the Internet. An updated relevant mobile responsive website for your firm is vital. Without this first part of a digital strategy in place, your business will become invisible. A LinkedIn profile help creates visibility It increases the visibility of your firm through Google searches. Most people searching the Internet do not go beyond page one of a search engine list. Every digital action you can take, however small, increases your visibility on the web. It then increases the potential of a client finding their way to your firm.

Does Traditional Advertising Still Have A Place?

The world of advertising has changed. How people find businesses has changed. Using directories such as Yellow Pages or Thomsons local is reducing. Just look how thick these directors are compared to the past. Do Funeral Directors still find new clients through advertising? Of course, there is still some place for traditional advertising. A large part of advertising budgets for most Funeral Directors are directories and newspapers. The number one question now to ask is how effective still is the advert? How many people saw that advert? As a standard process, ask clients where and how they found the information about your firm. It is simple market research. Set this up as an automated system for your administration department. How else, otherwise, do you know how effective your advertising is? You could be spending hundreds of pounds per month and not know if it is driving clients to your business.

What Makes Clients Chose Your Firm?

Funeral Directors often advertise in local newspapers because other Funeral Directors do the same. The question you need to ask, is why should someone choose your firm? Does your advert communicate everything a family wants to know? Are smiling staff next to shiny limousines enough for people to make an informed choice? A reputation of past service is of tremendous value to families who know your firm. An advert alone though does not speak to reputation. Your advert may say you are a"traditional family business." Is that enough information to make a choice? A web address on your traditional advert is invaluable. But the addition of a

LinkedIn icon on your traditional advert, could make all the difference for a client in choosing your firm. People recognise this symbol. It symbolises professionalism. People know it is possible to find out considerably more information about your firm. In a competitive marketplace, every advantage could make the difference in gaining a client.

How do you differentiate your firm from others in the area? There is a growing trend of national organisations buying up small family businesses. There are also many new and growing players in the marketplace. North East Lincolnshire Council voted to research how they could begin to arrange funerals.[35] They wanted to know if this could save them money and provide a service to the local community. The NAFD strongly responded to this proposal.[36] But it reveals that the future marketplace will change. What if similar local authorities consider the potential profitability of offering a funeral service? A BBC report says advertising of funeral services has radically changed in the last ten years.[37] To have considered advertising funerals on television would at one time have been unthinkable. It is now becoming commonplace with national organisations like Cooperative Funeral Care. The funeral industry is worth around £2bn annually in the UK. Many new opportunities are being identified and profitable businesses opened. All these points lead to the fact that traditional forms of gaining clients is changing. How will your firm respond to these changes? If trends are also true that the death rate is declining, it is even more important in a shrinking marketplace to be visible.

We All Want Choices About Everything

We live in a world of increasing choice. Buy a cup of coffee and notice how many choices you have to make! Take the complex and emotionally charged multiple choices when considering a funeral. That decision-making process is considerably difficult. People still want choices. When you provide information before a client reaches your door, it helps them choose. By having a LinkedIn profile, your business starts differentiating itself from other local firms. It is impossible for a family business to compete with the marketing strategy of national organisations. They have budgets of tens of thousands of pounds. However, families are looking for information and choices. You provide those choices when they look at your website and your LinkedIn profile. Having the LinkedIn profile provides the recognised professionalism of your business. It does this by profiling your experience, skills and services online as used globally by other professionals. It helps by giving more information to make a valued and considered choice. When you provide this option alongside traditional advertising, it increases the potential to guiding customers to your business. It builds a broader digital footprint which helps with search engine results when people are looking for information. That will be the mark of your businesses that maintains relevancy in a changing marketplace over the long haul. A LinkedIn profile guides clients to choose your firm by providing information, credibility and visibility.

3. A LinkedIn Profile Creates Growing Business Networks

As the adage goes, it is not what you know but who you know that matters! We all understand that that is not entirely correct, but it does have seeds of truth within it. Running a funeral business at its core involves relationships with people. To relate to different people in different situations is a vital skill. One minute you are discussing death certificates and coroner's reports with a doctor. The next is a conversation with a local florist who has chosen the wrong colour carnations. The door opens and a distraught family have come to discuss the arrangements for a funeral and they cannot remember the time that the celebrant is visiting them. Next, you are chasing a coffin manufacturer who promised he would deliver the handles yesterday. This complex web of managing different relationships could all take place in the space of a few minutes.

A Funeral Director needs to adapt to many different relationships when the situation demands. It is necessary to create, build and develop strong reciprocal relationships. There is the critical relationship between the Funeral Director and family. There are also significant and important relationships within the local community. It is key that ministers of religion and celebrants build positive relationships with Funeral Directors. A Funeral Director needs to develop strong links with significant partners in the area. This list is almost never-ending. It includes ministers, celebrants, florists, doctors, and printers. Say nothing of locations for funeral receptions, hospices and nursing homes.

Failing to spend time building and developing networks either aids or stymies business success. Invest a small amount of time building business networks through LinkedIn. It can save you hours and build healthy relationships in your community. Using LinkedIn helps by making local and regional professional connections online.

Many Funeral Directors belong to local networking groups. These could a Chamber of Commerce or organisations such as BNI. These are an effective means of building relationships and expanding your business network. They can be expensive both in time and money. A LinkedIn profile provides an opportunity to make and develop healthy relationships for free. LinkedIn helps you demonstrate professionalism, build a reputation and create visibility within the local community. A website alone, cannot do this.

There are many different approaches you can use to build connections through LinkedIn. LinkedIn's platform is available 24 hours a day. Most Funeral Directors are extremely busy. It is not always possible to find time to attend networking meetings. There is always, however, an odd 15 minutes in a day to connect with people online. Some down time where a short-term investment can lead to a long-term relationship profitability. LinkedIn provides that possibility.

How can you use LinkedIn to build networks? You can search for local connections. You could advertise your LinkedIn profile by adding the icon to your business card and your website. You can add connections when meeting suppliers or potential suppliers. By doing this regularly, over time, you build a vital and valuable support network. This is not a "quick fix approach. By investing time today, you will not see the benefits tomorrow or even within a month or two. The consistent and persistent process of using LinkedIn has significant compound impact over time.

Start by building an accurate personal profile. You need a profile that describes in detail your business and personal skills. What are you qualifications? How long have you been in business? What makes your firm unique? Do you serve on any funeral association boards? For example, some Funeral Directors are involved in charitable work. Highlight how you sponsor fund raising golf days. Alternatively, explain the ways that you support local hospice charities. All this information creates an active and interesting profile.

You can use your list of connections to gain access and introduction to other businesses. LinkedIn calls this second or third-degree connections. Want to get to know that new nursing home, or florists in the town? Is there anyone in your contacts who already knows them? LinkedIn can tell you that and then show you a path to gain an introduction to them. Are you looking for new staff? Searching for those people in your network may give you an opportunity to find the right someone.

When you have built strong LinkedIn networks, it provides you with an active invitation list. This is so valuable when the opportunity arises to request support. When we get a phone call out of the blue from a business connection asking for help, it can feel uncomfortable. Especially, if we have not heard from them for months. If, over a period, relationships

57

are developed, it is more likely our request for help will meet with a favourable reply. LinkedIn provides such an opportunity.

Using LinkedIn to create and build business connections, takes a small daily amount of effort. You respond to the notifications of a birthday. You send celebrations for a new job or change in position. LinkedIn sends you regular emails about such items. When you see an award or achievement, it provides an opportunity to congratulate someone. It never fails to amaze me how simple and powerful it can be to send a note of appreciation or congratulation. Most people value that connection and being noticed. LinkedIn provides you that opportunity on a regular basis. Within your business network, you can offer endorsements, recommendations and support. All these slowly but certainly build networks. This will be reciprocal. Here is a very important point to understand about the web - as in life if you are generous with praise and acknowledgement, it will be returned to you! Then when a prospective client looks at your LinkedIn profile they can see you are well connected. It builds respect in your local community. When local professionals in your community write recommendations, it enhances your credibility. If you want to build and develop strong networks in your community, invest time on LinkedIn. It will considerably assist in that process.

4. A LinkedIn Profile Identifies You As A Thought Leader.

What does it mean to be a "Thought Leader?" A "Thought Leader" is someone who is aware of new trends. Someone who sees changes in legislation and laws. They understand how they will have an impact on their marketplace. It is someone who is growing in their knowledge and experience. It is someone who shares this knowledge with other professionals. Why should this be of benefit to you? You may not have had considered this before. The benefit of sharing the latest news about the funeral industry sets you apart from other firms. It highlights your continued professional development. It says, "we are serious about our business."

How do you establish credibility as a Funeral Director? If you walk into a doctors surgery, it is normal practice to find certificates and diplomas on the wall. These establish a person's qualifications and skill in their area of knowledge. It provides a prospective patient with an unspoken sense of credibility. It creates trust. A Funeral Director holds the same level of professional status within a community. Displaying your membership of professional associations is important. However, most people would not understand the benefit of your qualifications. Likewise, displaying membership symbols on a website has some advantage. Most people will not choose to check out what they mean. A LinkedIn profile helps provide a Funeral Director with a bigger platform to display their credibility and skills.

LinkedIn provides many simple processes that can help identify your business as a "Thought Leader." LinkedIn Pulse[38] allows you to write short blogs on what is happening in the funeral industry. Being visible in the marketplace is growing in popularity and importance. Today consumers are more aware of online reputation in making decisions to buy. LinkedIn Pulse with its new app is an often underused and unutilised benefit, within a LinkedIn profile. It will take some time and creativity to build an expanding library of personal content. This investment will reap tremendous rewards over time. For example, write an article on prepaid funerals plans and it could drive many prospective clients to choose your firm.

LinkedIn lets you repost thoughts and ideas from other industry spokespeople. By frequently adding content, you prove you are a "Thought Leader." These simple activities establish a reputation. They demonstrate that you are aware of what is happening in your industry. It raises your professionalism, dedication and credibility. It is possible to maximise the use of such content by adding similar pages to your company's website. By doing this, it allows you to get the greatest benefit from the content you have created.

Alternatively, you could be commenting on the posts of other Funeral Directors. Doing this builds your reputation as someone who is current in their thinking about the industry. It is a tremendous advantage. First, professionals in your local community see you as someone who is growing and increasing in knowledge. It distinguishes you as being credible and professional. Second, for potential clients, it underlines and highlights that you are not just relying on your "family tradition." You are a progressive, relevant and effective business and spokesperson. These all create trust, reputation and credibility. All vital values that someone will identify and may influence his or her decision to choose your firm over one of your competitors.

Many Funeral Directors are committed to local organisations such as Rotary or Lions International. Some may sit on local council departments. A few minutes a week sharing local information or commenting on local issues also adds to building a strong reputation in your community.

Why bother? All these processes provide an added advantage over other businesses in your area. It could be the missing piece needed in a complex jigsaw puzzle of a decision to choose your firm over another. Why leave this to chance and perhaps the random noticing of an advert? If a Funeral Director takes the time to do these important but not urgent tasks, they provide a tremendous impact over the long haul. By being known locally as a "Thought Leader," it adds tremendously to your credibility. While these factors alone are not sufficient for someone's decision to choose your firm, they all add together. Using LinkedIn to create your reputation as a "thought leader" provides a huge benefit to the ongoing growth and profitability of the business.

5. A LinkedIn Profile Helps Sell "You" Before Selling Your "Business"

Why do people choose your business when they are looking for a Funeral Director? A significant factor in customers returning to the same Funeral Director is loyalty. They have used your firm in the past and now call on you again. However, that will not always be the same. The impact of the internet creates a situation where loyalty is no longer the deciding factor. The funeral industry marketplace continues to change. National companies are using more aggressive strategies to reach new customers. TV advertising and social media campaigns are becoming common place. A local Funeral Director needs new strategies to remain competitive and profitable.

What Are You Selling?

Do you consider that you are in the "selling" business? You receive an enquiry that asks the question, "how much will this funeral cost?" At this point, a sale begins. You will have met with this question hundreds of times before. You know what to say to move the conversation to a point of sale. The opening question is often about price. Experienced Funeral Directors understand there is far more at play here than just price. However, what happens if the customer does not make that call but searches about your business online?

How do you sell your business services? Is it on existing customer recommendations? Is it on good customer service alone? If so, what makes your funeral business different from others? What do you say when you are trying to convince a potential client to choose your firm? You may pride yourself on the conversion rate from phone call to obtaining the business. However, the way that people now buy everything has changed forever.

You may never have stopped to consider the words you use. Whatever you say, there is a sales process that is taking place. For that process to begin, somebody has to contact your firm. What about the many people who will be searching first through the Internet? How do you convince and sell your firm and the services you offer online? An updated mobile responsive website is the starting place of course. By having a LinkedIn profile, though, you add a strong link in the chain of information about your firm. It demonstrates professionalism; it builds a reputation, and it creates visibility.

How can LinkedIn help you create sales?

How can LinkedIn build sales? It is a proactive approach to build a sales process through LinkedIn. Many people do not agree that a funeral business can be "sold" as other service-based industries are. The marketplace has changed. There are new and creative initiatives around the subject of death. "Dying Awareness" week and "death cafes" create conversations about end of life choices. When they do, the first place people search for more information is the web. Another significant shift has taken place. People now want to have the financial and emotional choice for their end of life plans. The market for prepaid funeral plans creates profitable channels for a funeral business. These plans create an environment where people shop for your services in advance. It is a very different to a reactive choice when a loved one has passed away. Adding specific information about these products to your LinkedIn profile creates sales opportunities.

Dominic McGuire, from the Funeral Directors Association, sees the marketplace changing even more. He is quoted as saying, " In the past, most people would not even spot the Funeral Director's shop on the high street. The relationship between the sector and the public is changing. This is due in part to the introduction of pre-paid funeral plans." He estimates funeral plans will account for much of the industry's future market share. It will change the makeup of the sector itself.[39]

So How Will This Affect Your Business?

The fundamental underlying principle is the culture of choice that we live in today. People want choices. People want to control and have influence over the choices that affect their life and now their death. This is why there is significant growth in the marketplace for pre-paid funeral plans. With a funeral plan, you get what you want, not what your relatives may think that you want. Moreover, at a time you are unable to make those choices. It is an important choice to many people. The provision and advertising of selling this service will only increase. Your future clients will be shopping around on the internet to find this service.

Create a section on your LinkedIn profile about pre-paid plans. This allows you to sell yourself, before selling your services. You can show you are a "specialist" or "Thought Leader" in this area. This adds credibility when people view your business. This is selling in advance rather than selling for an event that has taken place. A LinkedIn profile creates a greater picture of professionalism as a Funeral Director. It raises your awareness and trust in a competitive marketplace.

How else can you sell your services online? Some forward thinking Funeral Directors have considered new forms of marketing their services. For example, paying for Google adverts and Facebook promotions. These provide a tremendous opportunity along with a potential minefield of problems. Recently, a man started to search for information following his diagnosis of cancer. He was bombarded with "adverts" from funeral companies.[40] This is inappropriate and disturbing for the person involved. Using social media has its benefits. Codes of practice for Funeral Directors and national organisations need to consider this area. There have also been classic "bad taste" adverts that have been selling funeral services. These include a large billboard in a subway station in New York. The firm was inviting people to "come a little closer" onto the tracks. This may not be the best way to drive new traffic to your business. Or, the thoughtless Florida-based funeral business, they added the firms address and logo to a cigarette lighter. It said, "Thank you for smoking!" These may raise a smile. Most professional Funeral Directors would not consider such advertising.

So what options does this leave? As discussed before directories and local newspapers are a source for advertising but their usefulness is dwindling. They have their place, but less and less so. Selling your services through LinkedIn gives you an edge. It gives you a competitive focus in a professional and relevant way. It allows you to sell you first. It helps sell your professionalism and sell your reputation before selling your services.

6. A LinkedIn Profile Helps You Respond To Changing Trends

In his famous quote Benjamin Franklin said, "In this world nothing can be said to be certain, except death and taxes."

He is right. The mortality rate is 100% and my tax assessment just came through the post! What we can also say, is nothing is certain about the future of the businesses that deal with death. How do you keep pace with this change?

National organisations produce regular magazines and articles relevant to the funeral industry. Most Funeral Directors read these magazines, gleaning odd snippets of information. This can be useful to help keep aware of what is happening. What can be far more effective is listen to conversations and chat with people in the same industry. People who are facing the same issues as you are day in and day out. Just watch as two Funeral Directors meet and how information and news passes. The recommendations we receive from people we know and trust sways our opinions. This perceived "trust" is a strange phenomenon. It exists as we often act on the recommendation that a friend has made. LinkedIn provides that opportunity for you to connect with other professionals across the world. It allows you to listen in or join in conversations with other people in the funeral industry. LinkedIn Groups is that feature.

LinkedIn Groups provide a daily stream of relevant articles, news and updates. As you scan the updates, you can learn what are the important topics of conversation today. What can you find there? In a recent scan, I noticed valuable information about many relevant issues. For example, there is increasing awareness and conversation taking place about digital legacies. How do you provide secure ways for passing on digital assets? Funeral Directors were talking about how they can discuss this area with clients. What they can say and how they can serve them better. There was a review of new websites using the Internet for mourning the loss of a loved one. Funeral Directors were reviewing these sites and considering how they could help their clients. All valuable information to help you stay current with the fast pace changes happening.

What about news? Click on the home button on a LinkedIn page and changing minute by minute is the latest news and articles. It provides quick bites of information. It provides short form news articles not crowded by adverts and promotions. For example, there are promotional items such as hiring a full-length trike-hearse. Alternatively, specific training courses you can join. These are firms who are looking for cars for sale and firms offering self-drive personal limo hire. These could be excellent leads and opportunities when you need them the most.

In the past, industry trends were just discussed in trade magazines and journals. This is no longer the case. All information is now in the public domain. Your clients will know about the digital services products and choices they can use. It is critical for a Funeral Director to know the changes the Internet is bringing to this sector. LinkedIn provides an accessible and up-to-date feed, so you are aware of any new trends. Moreover, not only awareness but how other professionals are responding to these trends.

Building reciprocal connections with other industry professionals creates the opportunity to pool knowledge. This knowledge is available daily rather than monthly through a trade magazine. LinkedIn assists you in keeping abreast of trends. By joining in and commenting on the discussions, it helps your business in the future. Taking just a few minutes a week scanning the list of shared knowledge puts you in a position of strength. It allows you to respond to a client when they ask your opinion of something new.

Another key benefit of LinkedIn is its global reach. Funeral Directors from around the world share ideas perhaps new to your market. How can you get an advantage in marketing your funeral business in your area? It could be possible to connect with a Funeral Director in Australia. Together you can be sharing new ideas without any fear of competition? There are a finite number of funerals each year. A growing number of companies are searching for that business. It is not hard to see how competitive the marketplace is becoming. Most Funeral Directors in an area know each other and have good working relationships. However, there will always be the underlying challenge of obtaining new business. You can gain a competitive edge as you adapt to new trends successful in other parts of the world. You too may be able to offer advice and strategies to help other Funeral Directors across the globe. This is an exciting and beneficial way of keeping up and in touch with new trends.

Currently, there are 235 open groups with "funeral" as a keyword. There are 128 closed groups that are only available to industry members. A simple click allows you to join and have access to a marketplace of industry professionals. Each one with differing views and opinions. Some you may just discount. Some could provide you with the knowledge that takes your business to the next level of effectiveness in this digital age. Moreover, it is all provided for free.

There are many other excellent resources for keeping abreast of the news and trends. I am not advocating that LinkedIn is the answer to all your needs for keeping your knowledge updated. What I am suggesting, is there is a significant benefit of investing time in a LinkedIn profile. It puts you at the heart of the latest news, discussions and issues. It allows you to build connections and take part in online conversations. It builds your online reputation. Why is this important? It is not uncommon now for people to investigate a company online before they use their services. A potential client sees you interested in providing the latest, relevant and innovative methods. Your online reputation shows you provide the highest quality of service to your clients. Potential customers can see your commitment to continual professional development and growth.

7. A LinkedIn Profile Allows You To Be Active In Professional Communities

The old proverb says, "birds of a feather, flock together." It is true! When people connected with a common cause or industry come together, they find a sense of camaraderie. I attended the 2015 National Funeral Exhibition. It is the showcase event for Britain's funeral industry held every two years. Major firms selling funeral products to the UK market consider this the premier event. It is an integral part of their sales campaign in the UK market. It is a trade only show. Those who are part of the funeral industry attend to see the latest products and services from their favourite suppliers. As well as established industries, innovative businesses were looking to open up sales opportunities. Many people spent time ambling up the different aisles. However, what was obvious to see was the rekindling of friendships. Friendly slaps on the back, hearty firm handshakes, and peals of laughter. This is common to see with people connected through their shared association with the funeral profession.

The major associations of Funeral Directors offer regular meetings and support events. Often, the pressures of work can make these beneficial and important times together secondary. Without doubt quality monthly magazines and e-newsletters provide the latest news and interesting information. However, there is nothing like chatting with someone who fully understands and has experienced a challenge that you may be facing. Learning firsthand how to deal with an issue when it arises, can save no end of research and worry. Connecting daily in professional communities helps your business and your development. You can have ready access to hundreds of other industry professionals at the click of a button. While it is not in "real" time, the value of "virtual time" is still of tremendous benefit. There are many advantages to being part of a LinkedIn professional community. It is a place where you can offer reciprocal support. Your experience and your skills could help another industry professional solve a problem. Professional networking can also help improve the success of your business. It allows you to connect with like-minded and experienced professionals.

Are you facing a challenge or issue that is new to you? Ask the question online in LinkedIn. It is certain that someone, somewhere has faced the same problem. They could help you save time, money and worry by answering the question. Alternatively, they could guide you towards the answer. Want to get something off your chest? Then here is a place where you can comment and get your views heard. The community can hear you, and you can start to bring about change. This opportunity for a voice is one of the amazing revolutions that the internet has brought to society. Where once it was almost impossible to have your say on some subjects, now you can. Multinational companies are brought to task because one person took the time to tweet a complaint. Now, through social media channels everyone can have a voice. There are the obvious extremes and negative outcomes of this channel of communication. The benefit to society is it gives a voice where before it was impossible to make your views known.

Beyond keeping abreast of news and you can become active and make an impression in industry groups in many ways. Start, by joining in conversations that are already taking place. If you see a recent update from another member, add a comment. It is easy to just "like" the post by clicking the thumb as in Facebook. This action is just saying, "I've noticed what you have said." It has little long term benefit beyond making the person who posted the content feel recognised. By writing a short comment, however, it raises your awareness in a community. Dr. Edmond Locard, the "Sherlock Holmes" of France, formulated the basic principle of forensic science.[41] Known as Locard's exchange principle, it says, "every contact leaves a trace." Nothing could be truer of this than on the internet. We leave a trace of being a "unique visitor" or "video view" or "follower" and those traces create attention, but not an impression. Why do so few people not take a moment to mention something positive by leaving a comment? Taking a few moments to type a couple of phrases after reading a post takes little time from our lives. Simple, short sentences take seconds to write. They acknowledge the author, which makes their day. (We all like to be noticed, don't we?) And it leaves a lasting positive impression on the recipient. Significantly, it leaves traces across the web associated with our names. Here is an important principle, **commenting creates influence.** By being part of conversations, it increases the number of people who will view your LinkedIn profile by upto four times.

Another way that you could make an impression is to create a regional group. You can be active in professional communities, especially in your location. Do you want to be seen as progressive and trend-setting as a funeral firm? Are you looking to expand your business in the future by purchasing other funeral businesses? Simple steps like these done consistently over time accumulate your presence on the web. It takes an investment of your time. It takes creativity. It takes effort. However, nothing in life that is of any value is any different.

In the resource section there is a list of funeral industry LinkedIn groups in the UK and around the world. A full search could find many more that focus on a specific aspect of the business. Start by selecting one or two major groups and become active in that community. Take a while to read the posts. Watch the etiquette of the group and then start to add comments of encouragement. Add value to the conversation taking place and it builds your professionalism, reputation and visibility on the web.

Why Don't More Funeral Businesses Use LinkedIn?

These seven powerful and productive ways build a strong digital footprint. By using LinkedIn, you **Demonstrate Professionalism**, **Build Reputation** and **Create Visibility**. You might ask, then, what is stopping businesses embracing this opportunity? That is the real question, and that is the reason that I have written this book! There are many great reasons for having a digital marketing plan. There are only a few reasons many funeral businesses do not. The questions and objections people usually raise fall into these four broad definitions.

- Lack Of Awareness

Everyone I speak to in the funeral industry is noticing the growing impact of the internet. That is not in dispute. What does comes to light, though, is a lack of understanding and knowledge. This subtle but disruptive online development has grown quietly in the background. However, it is starting to shout louder for attention. Traditional family run firms have operated the same way for many years. In some cases, for generations. Trading on reputation and using traditional forms of marketing worked well in the past. So why should they not work well in the future? They have, and to a point will continue to do so. The question is, will it be effective for the future marketplace? I am not advocating the abandonment of all what has worked well in the past. What I am encouraging, is that the funeral industry no longer relies on those old strategies. If you have read this far, you are not one of those people! You are someone interested in taking forward your business to a new level. You are someone interested in using the digital opportunities around you. Congratulations to you!

- **Lack of time**

This is a real and pressing issue for many people in business. How do I find the time to build this extra activity into my daily work schedule? Should I give this task to someone in the office or should I outsource this completely to another agency? It can be easy to find yourself spending an excessive amount of time on the web without even noticing it. Structured use of time on the internet can produce an inverse number of results for the investment of time. There are only so many hours in a day. Finding the most efficient way to spend that time is a crucial success in building any business. There is always the delicate balance between the issues of today and the customers of tomorrow. To ignore either is a long-term peril. For the success and profitability of a people-centred business both matter.

My question to this objection is, what is the alternative? Do you keep doing what you have always done? Do you stand by as more progressive and innovative funeral companies grasp the opportunity? Do you watch them build a bigger awareness for their business through digital marketing? It might not happen tomorrow. It may not be the day after or even next year, but the impact of Digitisation will be the eroding of your traditional marketing. The new customers of tomorrow will be found primarily through internet channels.

- **Lack of skill and knowledge**

This is a real problem and a pressing issue. I advocate that national associations should provide more training for their members. Not only the theory, but also skill-based coaching. In a non-regulated industry, there is no rule for continuous professional development. I am not suggesting national funeral associations neglect this area. Nothing could be more from the truth. They are always encouraging and providing members with opportunities to grow their professional knowledge. You rarely see in trade journals, the subject of digital marketing for businesses. Even in adverts and editorials seeing social icons for LinkedIn, Facebook or Twitter is a rarity. Some large regional funeral companies are breaking the mould. Simple yet creative use of social media sees them pulling away from the pack, pulling away from those firms who ignore bringing the Internet into the funeral business. In the reference section of this book, you will find some links to resources to educate yourself. My recommendation would also be to consider investing in some members of your staff. Invest in those who could learn and grow into this marketing opportunity. This staff can then be driving new customers long-term into your business.

- Lack of control

It is important that a business considers what their "voice" will be online. Issues of security, privacy and developing a social media policy are important areas. None of these should prevent your business engaging with existing or new customers online. Most of your staff are using social media today. Maybe it just needs considering how they use it in the workplace. It requires training, coaching and monitoring. It is important in dealing with sensitive issues with care to ensure appropriate responses. People understand now how connecting online with "friends," as in FaceBook keeps contact with many people. However, they are unsure how to go about using these same channels with business connections. This is where training and consulting are important. There are some great success stories of the impact of social media on business. However, also the odd horror story of how it went drastically wrong. So to let your staff loose without any guidance or training could be unwise. Please see the Action Steps Chapter for ways Death Goes Digital can help in consulting, training and coaching your team. As discussed earlier, the main three social media platforms are LinkedIn, Facebook and Twitter. These digital channels each have unique and creative ways for marketing online. Each uses special skills to build greater visibility for your business. The best place to start for any business, however, is LinkedIn.

Chapter Questions and Thought Provokers

- How much of your business is built on reputation and how much is driven by your marketing efforts?
- What systems do you have in place to know the source of your current clients?
- How do you display client testimonials in your business?
- What are your thoughts on regulating the funeral industry?
- How do you plan for your business to sell your services?
- How would you describe your uniqueness as a funeral business in your community?
- Why should someone choose your firm over a competitor?
- How do you keep up with trends and news about the funeral industry on a regular basis?
- How would you respond if your local council began to arrange funerals?
- What reputation does your business have with other professionals and suppliers?

Building A Personal Profile

"Nothing endures but change."

HERACLITUS

Building A Personal Profile

At the core of LinkedIn, is your personal profile. Your profile is like the "shop window" of your business when people find your website through a search. The adage sits true here, you never get a second chance to make a first impression. People will later judge you on your content. If the visual image on your profile page is weak, or irrelevant however, it could put people off contacting your business. The core message of this book is how important it is to have a LinkedIn profile. However, it is better to have no LinkedIn profile at all than an incomplete, or irrelevant profile. It is important that you complete this profile with the potential customer or business connection in mind. Getting the content right for this page is important. It must describe the **benefits** a customer receives from doing business with your organisation. This book is about the "why" rather than the "how" of LinkedIn. I will only cover the highlights here on completing a profile. There are many excellent Internet resources available to give help on completing a profile. Alternatively, you could outsource this part of the process. This could ensure completing it to the best possible standards. The resource section has more information on outsourcing a LinkedIn personal profile.

A LinkedIn profile is made up of many sections:

- Profile Header - An image at the top of your profile that adds a visual[42] representation of your business.
- Headline - This is the who you are and what you do.

- Personal Photo - People like to do business with a face. Have an up-to-date and professional looking photograph.
- Summary - A critical section that gives space to expand on your experience and the uniqueness of your business.
- Experience - Here you list the roles that you have had during your working career.
- Volunteer - This is where you can add links and information about the local charities you support for example.
- Honours and Awards - Have you or your firm been recognised for any achievement, either industry or local?
- Organisations - To which National or regional professional associations do you belong?
- Skills and Endorsements - This is a list of your top skills endorsed by others on LinkedIn.
- Education - What qualifications, diplomas, or degrees do you hold?
- Certifications - This is where you can display your industry specific skills.
- Recommendations - A list of specific individual reviews of you by people happy with your service or skills.
- Groups - Here is the list of connections you have in the industry and business groups.
- Publications - Have you written articles for trade magazines, local newspapers?

- Following - This is a list of all the companies that you are following on LinkedIn.

You can add other sections to build a comprehensive and professional picture of your business. Completing a LinkedIn profile takes time and effort. It needs thought and attention to detail to bring to life the uniqueness and benefits of doing business with your company. On first sight, you may think that this is just like an online CV. In some ways, it is. It can be more in depth by adding videos, images, and web links. These additions all help build professionalism, reputation and visibility for your business.

What makes a great LinkedIn profile? Jeff Bullas, a Digital Marketing strategist, recommends nine critical areas to make you stand out from the crowd. He cites areas such as using the correct pictures for the "Profile Header" a picture that sits at the top of your page. Your personal photograph, he says, needs to be chosen carefully. Mistakes people make are not using a picture at all. This immediately turns people away from your profile. Alternatively, choosing an photo of yourself that does not represent the professional status of your business. For example, pictures from your holiday in Spain or a photo from many years ago. While they may look good to you, the question is, does this look good to a potential customer? Remember that this profile is a personal reflection of you and your business. It is important you have a clear and compelling summary that describes what the benefits are of doing business with your firm. This is what most people will read first. Remember, this is not a place to list features. How old the company is, and how many new limousines you have, are not benefits. Think creatively about why somebody would want to do business with your firm. Pulling these words together takes time and effort. In the world of the Internet, they are "evergreen" content. Once completed, these main headings, unless something changes, will be there for a long time. Your personal profile needs to be rich with links to your website. Also, the National organisations you belong to and perhaps the local charities where you have fundraised. These all enhance your professionalism, reputation and visibility in the local community.

For more details read: 9 Steps to Creating A Powerful LinkedIn Profile[43] For a LinkedIn overview go to LinkedIn profile tips to bring your professional story to life. Other books and resources can help you further in completing a professional and comprehensive LinkedIn profile.[44]

Reading the above list with all the content that is required may, at first, seem daunting. Don't let inertia and procrastination stop you at this point! Most of the information will be available either in a resume or in your head. Allocate blocks of time to complete the profile. Alternatively, outsource the task to an agency who can create a professional profile for your business.

Building A Company Profile

"The people who resist change will be confronted by the growing number of people who see that better ways are available; thanks to technology."

BILL GATES

Building A Company Profile

What is the difference between a Personal and Company LinkedIn Profile?[45] A Personal Profile allows you to display your experience, skills and recommendations. A Company Profile is a place to provide an overview of your business. It is also a place to release news and information about what's happening in the business. Why have a Company Profile? There is a debate about how helpful and useful Company pages are on LinkedIn. In my opinion, there are many benefits of having a Company page, some that I highlight below.

It Allows Space To Tell Your Past, Present and Future story

"Once upon a time..." People love stories. There is something that engages our attention and draws us closer when we hear a story. Many Funeral Directors have wonderful stories of how the business developed over many generations of the family. Grandparents, great-grandparents and even great great grandparents built a reputable business over many years. Here is an opportunity for you to tell that story. Here is where you can prove the benefits of dealing with a long-established, local and trusted business. What is happening in your company right now? Are you planning to expand, move premises, or add new services? This is the section where you can make announcements about current news and also plans. Which means that people have an opportunity to gain a greater trust in the longevity of the business. By creating opportunities to tell the story of the past, the present, and the future, it all builds professionalism, reputation and visibility. Company updates can also be posted on the Profile.[46] Company updates are the news, opinions and announcements that the business makes to its community.

It Showcases Your Products and Services

A Company Profile allows you to create a master list of all your products and services. People want choice and want to know what services are on offer. A casual stroll down any supermarket aisle selling shampoo shows how much people want choice! A Company Profile allows you to list and add a description of all the services and products of your firm. This could be specialising in green funerals. Or, the availability of a motorcycle hearse or horse-drawn hearse for example. It is possible to add to these services media like videos and images. These give further information and help the professionalism and reputation of your firm.

It Builds Your Reputation By Displaying Your Staff's Skills.

Do you offer unique services in your area because of the skills of your staff team? Do you have a specialist in memorial jewellery? Do you have a staff member dedicated to green funerals? Do you have specialist embalming teams or on-site florists? Being able to link together all your employees in one centralised page, gives tremendous credibility to the service you can offer potential customers. A LinkedIn Company page provides that availability to your business. A company page allows you to link together staff under the name of your business. If you encourage your staff to engage and to connect online it speaks volumes about your company and your brand to anyone who visits your LinkedIn page.

It Allows You To Find Skilled and Experienced Employees

Are you looking to recruit new staff? By placing job opportunities on your company page, it allows professionals in the same industry to find your vacancies. Some Funeral Directors may be hesitant to encourage staff to network on LinkedIn. They fear that they may lose them as employees. Why? Because any savvy job seeker knows that they can use LinkedIn to network and establish their expertise in the funeral industry. They can search for new positions through LinkedIn. However, the higher visibility of your business, the better for Internet searches. It is better for customer reviews and better for finding and recruiting new staff.

For more details on building a presence for your business on LinkedIn by creating a Company Page check out LinkedIn Company Pages marketing solutions. [47] Alternatively, an excellent article, ten questions to ask when setting up a LinkedIn Company Page by Kim Lachance Shandrow in Entrepreneur magazine.[48]

Building Credibility Through Recommendations & Endorsements

"What people have the capacity to choose, they have the ability to change."

MADELEINE ALBRIGHT

Building Credibility Through Recommendations & Endorsements

From Amazon to Tripadvisor, the online review is integral to business visibility. Over the last ten years, posting reviews on purchases or services has become mainstream. The consumers opinion is of paramount importance. The collective voice of the customer can make businesses flourish or flounder. Though only a small proportion of the users of the Internet, are contributors, the comments of others influence significant percentages of the public. This development is called the "sharing economy."[49] Even the funeral industry will see the writing of online reviews grow over time. This aspect of business marketing will become embedded as a regular practice. It will be critical to the success of business in the future.

"More than 80% of consumers now check online reviews before making purchasing decisions." Says, Bill Tancer, the General Manager of global research for Experian Marketing Services.[50] In his opinion, failure to recognise and cultivate online reviews limits the uncapped opportunity available to businesses. This phenomenon should not be a surprise. Referrals and recommendations guide our decisions. The suggestions of the best local restaurant or food supplier have always influenced our buying decisions. In a recent survey, 92% of respondents reported that a positive recommendation from a friend, family member, or someone they trust is the biggest influence on whether they buy a product or service.[51] A transformational change has taken place. The unknown crowd are now influencing our decision

91

making. The Competition and Markets Authority (CMA) recently launched an investigation as to whether businesses even may be posing as satisfied customers just to boost their ratings![52]

How does this affect the funeral industry? In the past, most families return to Funeral Directors who handled the deaths of family members. If they were happy with the customer service no doubt, they would have commented to friends. The motto that a happy customer tells 12 other potential clients and an unhappy customer tells 24, if not accurate in numbers, is certainly correct in principle. How often do people have a meal in a restaurant that is not good, but when asked by their server, "Is everything ok?" Say, "yes, fine." Then go and tell everyone they know how bad the food was!

What if the family seeking a Funeral Director has no local history or connections? Turning to the local newspaper or Yellow Pages might find a Funeral Director. Now instead, people turn to the Internet. How can you know if that funeral business has a good reputation? Online reviews are providing that credibility and reputation. A professional profile on LinkedIn helps develop that positive consumer voice.

LinkedIn provides the possibility to request and receive recommendations. These are recommendations of your business from people within your network. This is why it is significant to build an ever increasing circle of business connections. Having relevant recommendations from suppliers, local ministers and past clients, for example, reinforces your company reputation.

How do you get recommendations? You need to ask! As discussed earlier, an essential step should always be the question, "How did you get to hear about us?" This is valuable information to uncover about what marketing methods are working. It also allows the opportunity to thank people who have recommended you. When when a client says, "I found you on the Internet," that should now start a new process. A critical step now involves connecting with that same customer in whichever online space they discovered your firm. By adding, "It is our standard business practice to connect with our clients through social media." So, it will not be a surprise later when you seek out and request connections with your customers.

Another way to get good-quality recommendations is to recommend others. Look through your existing suppliers, your local network and connections. Can you write short, relevant and specific recommendations for their LinkedIn page? Not only will they appreciate your positive support, but will likely return the recommendation. These simple but significant steps will aid the building of strong online recommendations. This builds trust. It works towards demonstrating professionalism, building a reputation and creating visibility for your business.

Adding Endorsements To Your LinkedIn Profile

LinkedIn also added a feature that allows users to endorse the skills of someone in their network. By using particular algorithms, LinkedIn generates a list of skills people could have. You can add to this list your skill set that people can endorse for your professionalism. There are many benefits

93

for this aspect of your LinkedIn profile. Rather than you declaring your abilities, others can give positive feedback on your skills. This carries far more credibility. Receiving endorsements from people in your network aids to building professionalism and demonstrating reputation. You could even ask someone who has endorsed your skills to write a recommendation! They all help build a solid and strong profile. Start by adding specific skills recognised as important from a customer perspective. It is possible to review and add more or hide skills that would not be important to display.

LinkedIn recommendations and endorsements serve to demonstrate that suppliers and clients value your business. Recommendations and endorsements help fulfil the central core tenant of this book. By developing and updating a professional profile on LinkedIn, you can demonstrate professionalism, build reputation and create visibility for your business in your community.

If you have read this far in the book, you will have learned the following:

- The three core reasons you need to implement Digitisation in your funeral business now.
- How Digitisation is bringing about significant change in how consumers think and search for information online about death and funeral planning.
- Why you should consider adding a LinkedIn profile to your digital footprint.
- The seven key benefits a LinkedIn profile adds to your business.

- What to include in a personal and company profile on LinkedIn.
- How online recommendations enhance your reputation and how to obtain them.

Conclusion

"What would life be if we had no courage to attempt anything?"

VINCENT VAN GOGH

Conclusion

My aim with this book was to encourage, educate and engage Funeral Directors around the subject of Digitisation and using LinkedIn. I hope that by now I have made a strong enough case to consider that doing nothing about Digitisation or LinkedIn is not an option.

"The only man who never makes mistakes is the man who never does anything." Benjamin Franklin

Could I have improved the writing of this book? Certainly. Could it have been longer, included more information or other topics, Quite possibly. There is always ways something that can be improved. However, perfection can be the biggest enemy of progress. We often do not do something because we worry what others will think. We fear that we might fail. We procrastinate and so nothing changes. I have not failed in the process of writing this book. There is no doubt that I have learned something in the process. Where I will feel I have failed is if you do nothing about the information it contains.

Take action.

Take action now.

Take action now with one small step.

Small actions done consistently produces dramatic results.[53]

Be brave and be bold to take a step in the direction of bringing Digitisation into your funeral business. If you do that, we both will have succeeded.

Thank you for reading this book. I hope that you have found it challenging and interesting. I would love to hear from you. Please write to me a info@deathgoesdigital.com

Next Steps - Take Action

How Can I Help You Implement The Lessons In This Book?

Book Peter Billingham As Keynote Speaker

I am an accomplished and engaging conference speaker. I have been speaking in public for many years and now mentor, train and develop other public speakers to grow their skills and businesses. By booking me as a conference speaker, you will get a professional and competent communicator on subjects relevant to the funeral industry. Visit the speaking page at www.deathgoesdigital.com to see a list of related speech topics and a form to hire me as a speaker.

Subscribe to Regular News and Updates

Death Goes Digital has a weekly Blog, will be starting a regular Podcast and gives you access to special offers for consulting and training to help your funeral business grow. If you want to know events where you will find me speaking, the best way to be first with the news is to sign up for the DGD newsletter on the website.

Join the Death Goes Digital Community

Bringing about change can be a lonely business. Those fateful words, "we've never done it that way before," can be the bell tolling the end of a company. Joining with others developing digitisation in the funeral business can help save time, create friendships and develop collaborative partnerships. For more information about joining the Death Goes Digital Community check out the community pages on the website.

Hire Peter Billingham As A Consultant

I work with a small number of clients as a consultant, coach and mentor. Having someone to guide you each step of the way through a process of change improves your chance of success. Together we set objectives for your business. Then face to face mentoring or using Skype, I help you navigate your way to use the internet to grow your funeral industry business. Mentoring can help you remain relevant in this changing marketplace. For more details of my consulting work see the Hire Me As A Consultant Page on the website.

Outsource The Creation Of Your LinkedIn Profile or Social Media Marketing

Would like to build a profile online through LinkedIn? Do you not have the time or feel you have the skills to do this? Then outsource that project to Death Goes Digital. We can offer you a professional review of your current digital impact. We can write your profile for LinkedIn, establish social media channels and provide training or monthly social media creation packages. If you are interesting in learning more how we can help you specifically, please write to info@deathgoesdigital.com and let's start a conversation.

Let's Connect On LinkedIn

Send a connection request with the email info@deathgoesdigital.com - https://uk.linkedin.com/in/peterbillingham

About Peter Billingham

Peter Billingham has been involved in building organisations as a leader, coach and entrepreneur for more than 30 years. A skilled and engaging communicator at heart, Peter understands how businesses can harness the power of social media to promote and grow a business. More importantly, Peter has built national and international organisations on the strength and knowledge of effective, creative leadership and the powerful use of digital media strategies.

An author, speechwriter and professional public speaker, Peter has the skills and knowledge to coach business owners and entrepreneurs to higher levels of productivity and effectiveness in communication and the use of digital platforms. Along with speech writing, Peter coaches CEO's, Senior Managers and entrepreneurs on public speaking skills. Peter is an Enterprise Market Place Nation Growth Voucher Advisor for developing digital strategies for businesses. He holds the role of President for Heart of England Toastmasters Club and speaks regularly at media conferences and leadership training events.

Peter has a small number of clients he works with as a consultant, coach and mentor. Having someone to guide you each step of the way through a process of change improves your chance of success. Together he sets objectives for your business. Then through face to face mentoring or using Skype, he helps you navigate your way to use the internet to grow your funeral industry business. This helps you remain relevant in this changing marketplace. Here is what clients say about his consulting work.

"Peter is one of the most superb Executive Coaches out there. Most impressive and inspiring is that he models what he says. He is focused, organised and single-minded in his pursuit of excellence, and has a knack of bringing this out in teams and individuals. Personally I have benefited from working alongside him for a number of years, observing his leadership and seeking to emulate it. I also received direct coaching on numerous occasions in preparing presentations and public speaking, and this is where Peter's strengths really come to the fore."

-- Andrew Flynn - Head of Research and Data Analysis at Christian Vision

"Peter was very effective when we engaged him as a Consultant to advise Storwell Systems Ltd and assess our Social Media Activities to improve them. In particular, Peter identified tools and specific strategies that helped focus our efforts to get best outcomes. Our new Graduate recruit was given one to one coaching over a number of weeks which helped him to understand the process and raise the quality of his work. Some great quick wins and many more lasting lessons which we have adopted.

-- Sanat Shelat - Storwell Systems Ltd"

Peter is an AOIC (Association of Independent Celebrants) Celebrant in Worcestershire and the West Midlands through his celebrant business called Memorable Words.

Why Memorable Words? Memorable words was started with the vision and mission in mind to create end of life services that are unique, individual and relevant. Peter believes that in his role as a celebrant it is a honour and privilege to conduct and officiate at the funeral of somebody's loved one. Peter wanted to help families by working together to design a celebration of the loved ones life that is full of comfort, hope and memorable words. Underlying his work with clients is the mission of Memorable Words:

- 7 Billion people are currently living on earth
- Each one is unique
- When a life ends, words are usually spoken.
- We believe those word should be unique and memorable.

Memorable Words works in Bromsgrove, Droitwich, Redditch, Kidderminster and the surrounding areas providing Independent Funeral Celebrant services.

For more information visit www.memorablewords.co.uk

You can find out more about Peter Billingham or Death Goes Digital at:

Death Goes Digital

Website: www.deathgoesdigital.com
Twitter: @DeathGoesD

Peter Billingham

The Artful Speaker Website - www.Peterbillingham.com
LinkedIn Profile - https://www.linkedin.com/in/peterbillingham
Twitter - https://twitter.com/PeteBillingham

Resources:

Listed below are some resources and recommendations that I have found useful in studying and using LinkedIn as a business networking tool. These are just some of resources available, a simple search on the Internet will deliver significant and specific results.

LinkedIn Help Centre - This portal provides resources, tutorials and case studies for every aspect of setting up and building a network through LinkedIn. This should be the first call for learning about LinkedIn and the **features** it contains. https://help.linkedin.com/

LinkedIn on YouTube - This resource is a wealth of tutorials, explanations and further studies about using LinkedIn to build business networks. There are many videos on all aspects of using and getting the most from a professional profile on the social networking site. https://www.youtube.com/user/LinkedIn/videos

Both of the above hold most of the information you may require and have free access to view the information.

According to Amazon UK there are over 3000 books on LinkedIn or connected with using LinkedIn as a business. One of my favourites because of its ease of access and easy reading style is LinkedIn For Dummies by Joel Elad.

Websites:

Wayne Breithbarth has an excellent list of free resources on how to get more out of LinkedIn in various areas on his website - http://www.powerformula.net/

See also http://www.powerformula.net/free-resources-for-learning-linkedin/

Blogs:

LinkedIn Official Blog - http://blog.linkedin.com/

Linked Into Business by Viveka von Rosen - http://linkedintobusiness.com

Alltop - an aggregator of web content has a special LinkedIn feed - http://linkedin.alltop.com/

Notes

[1] For more information and to view the TED talk, "Want To Be Happy? Be Grateful view http://on.ted.com/gratefulness

[2] BOLD - How To Go Big, Create Wealth and Impact The World. Peter H. Diamandis and Steven Kotler. Published by Simon and Schuster 2015

[3] BOLD - How To Go Big, Create Wealth and Impact The World. Peter H. Diamandis and Steven Kotler. Published by Simon and Schuster 2015 p.10

[4] See - https://director.funeralbooker.com/

[5] https://www.sunlifedirect.co.uk/press-office/cost-of-dying-2015/

[6] http://www.royallondon.com/about/media/news/2014/october/new-study-reveals-scale-of-funeral-poverty-uk-funeral-debt-reaches-142m/

[7] Apple's Think Different advertising campaign. 1997-2002

[8] Digital Evolution - Learning from leaders in digital transformation. The Economist Intelligence Unit Limited 2015

[9] The reference section of this book lists other ways you can learn and explore more of the features of LinkedIn.

[10] http://www.nelincs.gov.uk/news/2015/mar/delivering-differently/

[11] Merriam Webster Dictionary
http://www.merriam-webster.com/dictionary/professionalism

[12] Quoted in "The BadCost of Customer Service" by Help Scout
http://www.helpscout.net/75-customer-service-facts-quotes-statistics/

[13] Dictionary.Com
http://dictionary.reference.com/browse/reputation

[14] What is reputation management?
http://en.wikipedia.org/wiki/Reputation_management

[15] http://dictionary.reference.com/browse/visibility

[16] USA Today -
http://usatoday30.usatoday.com/news/nation/death-goes-digital

[17] Legacy.com - Where Life Stories Live On
http://www.legacy.com/ns/

[18] Dying Matters is a coalition of 30,000 members across England whiles which aims to help people talk more openly about dying, death and bereavement, and to make plans for the end of life. http://www.dyingmatters.org/

[19] Each year in May Dying Matters and their coalition members host a fantastic range of events and activities around the country with the aim of getting people talking about death, dying and bereavement. In 2015 the theme is Talk, Plan, Live. For more information visit the website at: http://www.dyingmatters.org/YODOlaunch2015

[20] C.P.J. Field & Co Ltd
http://www.cpjfield.co.uk/marketing/writer-in-residence/
Interestingly, they have a very professional LinkedIn profile for their funeral services Company and an excellent website. https://www.linkedin.com/company/c.p.j.-field-&-co.-ltd.

[21] Confessions of a Funeral Director is a fascinating study of how one funeral firm is using the Internet to grow their business.
http://www.calebwilde.com/

[22] University of Bath, Centre for Death & Society
http://www.bath.ac.uk/cdas/

[23] Appitized Funeral App Specialists - the official app partner of the NAFD http://funeralcareapps.com/

[24] For an excellent article to download on this subject go to http://www.saga.co.uk/legal/everyday-legal/digital-legacy.aspx

[25] For more information on the history and current use of LinkedIn see: https://press.linkedin.com/about-linkedin

[26] https://www.linkedin.com/static?key=what_is_linkedin

[27] Conducted March 2015

[28] OFT internal review of funeral industry quoted in http://powerbase.info/index.php/Funeral_Industry

[29] According to Jeffbullas.com - http://www.jeffbullas.com/2015/02/18/9-steps-creating-powerful-linkedin-profile/#gVK2q3EEP3GP7p3a.99

[30] An excellent source on the current use and demographics on LinkedIn is the annual LinkedIn survey by Wayne Breitbarth. In 2014 896 active users were surveyed from around the world. For a detail analysis of the findings in an infographic format see: http://www.powerformula.net/linkedin-infographic-portrait-of-a-linkedin-user-2014/

[31] For more information see http://expandedramblings.com/ and specifically on the use of LinkedIn this page http://expandedramblings.com/index.php/by-the-numbers-a-few-important-linkedin-stats/

[32] http://stakeholders.ofcom.org.uk/binaries/research/tv-research/news/2014/News_Report_2014.pdf

[33] http://www.independent.co.uk/news/media/press/the-dizzying-decline-of-britains-local-newspapers-do-you-want-the-bad-news-or-the-good-news-9702684.html

[34] The Good Funeral Guide website has a growing and comprehensive list of vetted and recommended funeral directors with the facility for customer reviews to be added. For more information see : http://www.goodfuneralguide.co.uk/funeral-directors/

[35] http://www.nelincs.gov.uk/news/2015/mar/delivering-differently/

[36] http://www.nafd.org.uk/2015/03/10/the-nafd-responds-to-north-east-lincs-council-plans-to-offer-funeral-services

[37] http://news.bbc.co.uk/today/hi/today/newsid_9324000/9324262.stm

[38] https://www.pulse.me/

[39] http://www.mlmsolutions.co.uk/Blog/debt-help-for-businesses/is-the-funeral-industry-a-dead-certainty-for-smes.html

[40] http://www.dailymail.co.uk/sciencetech/article-2989768/Facebook-slammed-advertising-funeral-directors-CANCER-patient-Promotions-appeared-sufferer-Googled-disease.html

[41] https://en.wikipedia.org/wiki/Edmond_Locard

[42] Viveka Von Rosen writes an excellent article on the Social Media Examiner Blog on how to create an eye catching profile header - http://www.socialmediaexaminer.com/new-linkedin-header-image/ There are also many excellent resources on her website: http://linkedintobusiness.com/

[43] http://www.jeffbullas.com/2015/02/18/9-steps-creating-powerful-linkedin-profile/#gVK2q3EEP3GP7p3a.99

[44] https://smallbusiness.linkedin.com/professional-branding/linkedin-profile-tips

[45] For a detailed PDF on how to build a Company Page see: https://business.linkedin.com/content/dam/business/marketing-solutions/global/en_US/site/pdf/cs/linkedin_company_pages_guide_us_en_130314.pdf

[46] See 15 Tips for Compelling Company Updates: https://business.linkedin.com/content/dam/business/marketing-solutions/global/en_US/site/subsites/content-marketing/img/V2/e3_Infographic_Draft_11_1200.pdf

[47] Building a Company Profile - https://business.linkedin.com/marketing-solutions/company-pages/get-started

[48] Kim Lachance Shandrow - 10 Questions To Ask When Setting Up A LinkedIn Company Page: http://www.entrepreneur.com/article/226637

[49] https://en.wikipedia.org/wiki/Sharing_economy

[50] http://www.billtancer.com/

[51] Paul M. Rand, Highly Recommended: Harnessing the Power of Word of Mouth and Social Media to Build Your Brand and Your Business

[52] http://www.marketingmagazine.co.uk/article/1352230/brands-investigated-bashing-competitors-fake-online-reviews

[53] For more ideas on taking small action steps see - One Small Step Can Change Your Life: The Kaizen Way by Robert Maurer

Made in the USA
Charleston, SC
11 August 2016